MALFUZAT

Utterances Of Shaikh Abdul-Qadir Jilani

(May Allah be pleased with him)

Tr. By: Shaikh Muhammad ibn Yahya at-Tadifi al-Hanbalion

KITAB BHAVAN
New Delhi - 110 002 (INDIA)

Name of the book : Malfuzat - Utterances of Shaikh Abdul Qadir Jilani

Written by : Shaikh Abdul Qadir Jilani

Translated by : Shaikh Muhammad ibn Yahya at-Tadifi al-Hanbalion

2nd Edition : 2017

ISBN : 81-7151-390-5

Book Code : M00065

Printed & Published by: Nusrat Ali Nasri for Kitab Bhavan
Moonis Ali Nasri for Kitab Bhavan
1784, Kalan Mahal, Darya Ganj, New Delhi-110002

PRINTED IN INDIA

If you have any corrections, comments, or questions about this publication, please feel free to contact us.

CONTENTS

MALFUZAT -1

ON VIGIL

The Shaikh (may Allah be well pleased with him) also spoke about His words (Exalted is He):

Keeping vigil by night is more potent in impact. (73:6)

This refers not only to giving up sleep in the ordinary sense, but also to giving up the sleep of involvement with creatures, the lower self [nafs], natural inclination [tab'], passion [hawa] and wilfulness [irada]. For its food and drink the heart is left with speaking confidentially [munajat] to Allah (Almighty and Glorious is He), standing [qiyam] and bowing [ruku'] and making prostration [sujud] in His presence.

Surely you can see that if someone abstains from this world, so as not to be distracted by it from seeking the Lord of Truth (Almighty and Glorious is He), he must likewise abstain from the hereafter, so that it will not distract him from Allah (Almighty and Glorious is He). He must wish that the hereafter did not exist, because it is so charming, such an obvious mercy. He must make the heart and the innermost being become a face, on the surface of which the contents of his heart are visible. He must want this world to last, because he is worshipping Allah in secret, doing business with Him in secret.

You are in isolation from the Lord of Truth (Almighty and Glorious is He). When will you isolate your heart from creatures and seek the company of the Lord of Truth, going from door to door until there is no door left, from town to town, from heaven to heaven until there is no heaven left?

He [the believer] will bring the Resurrection upon himself. He will stand before the Lord of Truth (Almighty and Glorious is He), reading the records of his deeds, the good and the bad which consign him to the Fire [of Hell]. While he is caught between fear and hope, between falling into the Fire and crossing over it, Allah (Exalted is He) will overtake him with His gracious kindness. He will put out the Fire with the water of His mercy, and the Fire will exclaim: "Pass through, O believer [mu'min], since your light has extinguished my flames!" The passage–a journey that should take three thousand years–will be shortened for him to an instant, and then, when he is near to the palace of the King, he will recover his senses, his volition, his love for His Master [Mawla] and his ardent longing for Him. He will say: "I shall not enter except in the company of the Beloved [Mahbub]."

Do you not see? [As we know from sayings of the Prophet (Allah bless him and give him peace)], the miscarried foetus [siqt] will halt at the door of the Garden [of Paradise], saying: "I shall not enter until my parents enter. Where is the neighbour? Where is the witness?"

He will not enter until he is touched by the hand of the Prophet (Allah bless him and give him peace) and he can go in to meet the Beloved. Then, when he has finally experienced this, he will be sent back into this world, in order to receive his full quota of the shares allotted by destiny [aqsam], so that the [divine] foreknowledge ['ilm] shall not be altered, abrogated and annulled. Your Lord has finished with the work of creation.

[As the Prophet (Allah bless him and give him peace) has said:]

No soul shall depart from this world until it has received its allotted share [qism] in full.

You must therefore be dutifully devoted to Allah (Almighty and Glorious is He) and have the decency to look to the Lord of Truth for what you need, instead of to His creatures. The material means [asbab] are a screen.

The King's doors are locked. If you turn away from them, there will be opened unto you a door you can recognize. The door of the innermost being has swung shut [babu's-sirri sara ila sadd], but then it is opened without your own power and strength.

The believer [mu'min] must leave his natural inclination [tab'] behind, moving in the direction of his Lord. As long as he is following this present course, he is exposed to harmful influences affecting his person and his property. He is reverting to his sins, to his bad behaviour and to infringing the rules [hudud] of the sacred law [shar'] of his Lord. He must not seek help through supplication [du'a'], nor must he seek help from anyone other than his Lord. No, he must remember his sins and practice self-criticism until, when he has done a thorough job of this, he can resort to acceptance of the decree of destiny [qadar], to surrender [taslim] and entrustment [tafwid] as far as his heart is concerned. Once he is in this state, he will see an open door.

Whoever is dutiful toward Allah, He prepares a way out for him. (65:2)

He puts His servant to the test to see how he will behave:

And We have put them to the test with good things and bad things. (7:168)

The heart of the son of Adam must continue to travel along the path of good and evil, honour and humiliation, wealth and poverty, until he finally acknowledges that all blessings are due to Allah (Almighty and Glorious is He). This means gratitude [shukr]-and gratitude is an act of obedience [ta'a] performed without moving the tongue and the limbs of the body-and patient endurance of misfortune. He must admit his sins and offences until, having taken his last step on the good side and his last step on the bad side, there he is at the King's door. He has taken the step of gratitude and the step of patience, with divine help [tawfiq] as the guide. He has seen the King's door, and beyond it he can see things that no eye ever saw, that no ear ever heard of, and that never occurred to any human heart. The alternating sequence of good moves and bad moves is at an end; now comes the turn of conversation, discourse and sitting in company [with the Lord].

Can you grasp this, O 'Iraqi, O camel at the mill, O stupid fool? You go through the motions of ritual prayer [anta fi qiyam wa-qu'ud] without sincerity. You perform the prayers [tusalli] for the sake of other people, and while you are fasting [tasumu] your eyes are on their dishes of food and on the contents of their houses.

O alien to the human race, O straggler from the ranks of the champions of truth [siddiqun] and the Lord's own people [rabbaniyyun]! Do you not realize that I am your goldsmith's furnace, your probe and your touchstone? Do your utmost. Refuse to let me eat from your plate. Unsheathe your sword against me. You do not amount to anything. O little ignoramus, I am twisting your reins. I am giving you good advice and treating you with compassion. I am afraid that you may die an atheist [zindiq], a pretender [mura'i], an impostor [dajjal]-doomed to suffer in your grave the punishment of the hypocrites [munafiqun]. So you must desist from what you are up to. You must strip yourself naked and then put on the clothes of dutiful devotion [taqwa]. You will soon be dead. There is no hostility between me and you. You will have cause to remember what I am saying to you.

The insight of the righteous man [salih] is indicative of his spiritual state [hal]. When someone really knows ['arafa] Allah, his tongue falls silent; he is free from want because of Him, and of Him alone he is in need.

In my childhood, back in my home town, I used to hear someone saying to me, "O blessed one [ya mubarak]." I would run away from that voice, but then in solitude I would hear someone saying to me: "I think well of you."

If you wish for success [falah] you must stick close to me. When you see a person running away from me, you must know that he is a hypocrite.

The believer [mu'min] is such that, when he closes the eyes in his head, the eyes of his heart are opened and he sees what is over there; and when he closes the eyes of his heart, the eyes in his head are opened and he sees the situation of Allah and His dealings with His creatures.

The words of Allah addressed to Moses (peace be upon him) include the following:

I have chosen you above all men to receive My mission and My words. (7:144)

"And I have drawn you close to Me. One day you were shepherding a flock of sheep when one of them strayed off, so you followed after it until you caught up with it. By then you were exhausted, as it was exhausted, so you picked it up and hugged it and you said: 'You have worn yourself out and you have worn me out.'"

The remedy for someone who is separated [from the Lord] is detecting the cause of his separation, turning from it in repentance and confessing it in His presence.

The sinless ones [ma'sumun], those who are protected from every aspect, they do not have creative power [takwin]. Creative power comes in the process of following the path [fi't-tariq]. There is nothing worth talking about until you cross the wastelands, the deserts, the two continents and the two oceans -the continent of creatures and the continent of the self [nafs], the ocean of the law [hukm] and the ocean of knowledge ['ilm] -as well as the shore.

For the people [of the Lord] there is neither night nor day. Their diet is the diet of the sick and their sleep is the sleep of the drowned. Their speech is only out of necessity. When someone really knows Allah, his tongue falls silent, but "when He wills, He resurrects him" (80:22), and then he speaks without instruments, without tools, without preparation, without time for thought, without pretext. There is no difference between his tongue and his finger. Thus there is no wall of separation, no restriction, no door and no doorman, no permission to be granted or sought, no authorization and no dismissal, no Satan and no sultan, no inner core [janan] and no fingertips [banan].

MALFUZAT-2
ON DEVOTING ONESELF TO ALLAH

The Shaikh (may Allah be well pleased with him) also said, concerning the story of Moses (peace be upon him):

The innermost being [sirr] is the secret of the mystery [sirru's-sirr]. He left his family when he noticed a fire in the direction of the mountain. What did he see? The eye of the head saw a fire [nar], while the eye of the heart saw a light [nur]. The eye of the head saw a creation [khalqan], while the eye of the heart saw a Divine Truth [haqqan].

He said to his household: "Stay here awhile, I notice a fire." (28:29)

It attracted him through his heart, and disposed him to relinquish control of his wife and his children.

"He said to his household, 'Stay here awhile...'" A summons has come from on high. The grappling irons of destiny have snatched the people [of the Lord] away from their wives and their children. O law [hukm], stay in place! O knowledge ['ilm], advance in the name of Allah! O lower self [nafs], stay in place! O heart [qalb] and innermost being [sirr], respond! What a loser is he who fails to grasp this, who does not love this, who does not believe in this! How great his loss, how great his loss! How far apart he must remain! How terrible for him!

Perhaps I shall bring you news of it. (28:29)

"Stay there where you are, until I bring you news of the path." Because he had in fact strayed from the path. Its signposts were out of his sight. The Archangel [naqib an-nuqaba'] appeared in his presence, although it had never appeared to him before then. As it beckoned to him, it said: "You must wish you had never been created, and that, having been created, you knew what you had been created for!"

O sleeper, you must wake up, for the waters of the flood are all around you. Who is your leader [imam]? On the Day of Resurrection you will be called to give evidence. What is your Scripture [kitab]? Who is your teacher [mu'allim]? Who is your summoner [da'i]? Who is your Prophet [nabi]? You have no noble lineage [nasab]. Those whose lineage is authentic in the sight of Allah and in the eyes of His Prophet (Allah bless him and give him peace) are the people of dutiful devotion [ahl at-taqwa]. "O Messenger of Allah," someone asked, "who are members of your family?" The Prophet (Allah bless him and give him peace) replied:

Every dutiful believer belongs to the family of Muhammad [kullu taqiyyin alu Muhammadin].

Hold your tongue, you have no common sense! Your house sits on the River Tigris and yet you are dying of thirst. Just two steps and you would reach the All-Merciful [ar-Rahman]. The lower self [nafs] and creatures [are the two things you need to step away from]. You too, O seeker! Just two steps and you would reach your goal in both this world and the hereafter.

If you wish for success [falah], you must endure with patience the hammer blows of my way of speaking. When my ecstasy [junun] overtakes me, I cannot see you. When the temper [tab'] of my innermost being [sirr] is aroused, the temper of my sincerity [ikhlas], I cannot see your face. I wish to improve you and to remove the dross from your heart. I shall put out the fire [hariq] that threatens to burn your house down, and I shall protect the honour of your womenfolk [harim].

Open your eyes and take notice of what is in front of you. The squads of punishment and chastisement have come to get you. Woe unto you, O stupid fool! You will very soon be dead. All that you are now involved in must fade away and be scattered. This fellow here will have to part [yufariqu] with his children, his home and his wife, and then make friends [yurafiqu] with the dust, the grave, and either the stokers of Hell [zabaniya] or the angels of mercy [mala'ikat ar-rahma]. O passing traveller, O transient, O transferee, O temporary loan!

Glory be to the One who treats you all so kindly [subhana man manna 'alaikum], O you who like to have fun without ever taking notice!

O you who forget your friends, not once a year do you bring me the tiniest trifle, let alone once a month or once a week. Take something for nothing, and tomorrow a million things. I am carrying your burdens, while you are scared that I might give you the job of bearing mine. Only Allah (Almighty and Glorious is He) can take care of all my needs.

You say you would travel for a thousand years just to hear one word from me? But why, when the distance between me and you is only a few steps? You are lazy. You are a little ignoramus, a silly little fool. You think you have something to give. How many like you this world has fattened and then devoured! It made them plump with fame and fortune, then ate them up. If we had seen any good in it, you would not have beaten us to it.

Do not all things come home to Allah? (42:53)

As for what we are involved in, it all comes from Allah (Exalted is He).

When the Shaikh had stepped down from the lectern, one of his pupils [talamidha] said to him: "You were quite extreme in your admonition, and you spoke to him very harshly!" But the Shaikh replied: "If my words have had any effect upon him, he will surely come back for more." (The man did in fact attend the meeting [majlis] regularly from then on. He would also visit the Shaikh at other times, outside the formal session, and always behaved with the utmost humility and modesty in his presence. May Allah the Exalted bestow His mercy upon him.)

O Allah [grant us] patience and pardon! O Allah, help us!

If you stand in the presence of any fellow creature, trying to obtain what he has at his disposal, Allah will despise you.

As the Prophet (Allah bless him and give him peace) has said:

When someone pesters [tada'da'a] a rich man, seeking what he has in his possession, two thirds of his religion are gone.

You have made a habit of trying to scrounge things from your fellow creatures, so you will be in that condition when you have to meet Allah (Exalted is He). One time in the public square I saw a man scrounging from the people, although he had just sold a jubba of silk brocade for twenty-five dinars [gold coins]. So I followed him. He stopped beside a man who was eating harisa, and would not leave him alone until he gave him a mouthful of it. I said to him: "Did you not sell a jubba for such and such a price?" His response was: "I am neglecting my trade because of you!"

When someone has progressed to the ultimate degree of saint-ship [wilaya], he becomes a Qutb [spiritual axis, pole or pivot]. As such, he must carry the burdens of all creatures put together, but he is given the equivalent of the faith [iman] of all creatures put together, so that he will have the strength to bear what he must bear.

Pay no attention to my long shirt and my head-cloth. This is what one wears after death. This is a shroud [kafan], the shroud of the dead. This is what befits me now, after I have been accustomed to wearing coarse wool [suf] and to eating rough or going hungry. I now have a pressing engagement, but not with any of you.

O people of Baghdad, be sensible! O people of the earth, O people of the heavens!

And He creates what you do not know. (16:8)

It is not an affectation. This is an outward appearance [zahir] that has an inner content [batin] to prove its authenticity, and an inner reality that has an outer manifestation to confirm it.

There is nothing worth talking about until your lords [arbab] become one single Lord [Rabb], until your interests become single and the object of your love becomes single. Your heart must be unified. When will the nearness of the Lord of Truth pitch its tent in your heart? When will your heart come to be enraptured [majdhub] and your innermost being [sirr] drawn near [muqarrab], and when will you meet your Lord after taking your leave of creatures?

As Allah's Messenger (Allah bless him and give him peace) has said:

If someone devotes himself entirely to Allah (Almighty and Glorious is He), He will provide him with everything he needs, and if a person devotes himself entirely to this world, Allah will leave him in its care.

[In the first of these cases], things will occur miraculously [tukhraqu'l-'adat] for his benefit. He will receive what Allah has at His disposal, but only after total dedication to Him with his heart and his entire being [kulliyya].

As Allah (Exalted is He) has said:

If anyone performs an action with the intention of involving someone other than Me [as a partner] in it, well, I am the more Independent of the two partners [ana aghna'sh-sharikain]. It [the action] involves the partner ascribed to Me [shariki] and has nothing to do with Me.

Sincerity [ikhlas] is the believer's plot of land, while his deeds [a'mal] are its surrounding walls. The walls are subject to alteration and change, but not so the ground. Only upon dutiful devotion [taqwa] can a building be firmly based.

If someone should say: "I have dedicated myself to Allah (Almighty and Glorious is He), but He has not provided me with everything I need," the answer must be: "The fault lies in you, not in the Messenger."

Nor does he [the Messenger] speak from his own desire. (53:3)

Do you know anything at all about Allah (Exalted is He)? No, by Allah! You are all madly in love with this world and its glamour. If you were telling the truth about the claims you make, you would not have to resort to cunning tricks in order to obtain the merest trifle.

Cast your lower self [nafs] into the Valley of Destiny [wadi'l-qadar] until, when its time has come, the top rung of your ladder makes contact with the door of nearness [to the Lord]. You will be welcomed by a face more lovely than all the charming beauty of this world and the hereafter. The fond affection [mawadda] between the pair of you will be complete. All obstacles and intermediaries will disappear. Then you will hear its [the lower self's] call for help from the Valley of His Destiny: "Take charge of the deposits held in trust for you, and make full use of the service I can offer you. I am imprisoned over here, to your detriment or for your benefit." Your nearness [to the Lord] will plead on its behalf, urging a positive response to its request. At this point the hand of knowledge ['ilm] will be extended to it, and the hand of the law [hukm] will come to its aid.

As for your immersion in it [this world] at the outset of your career, before you have mounted any opposition to your natural urges [tab'], your passions [hawa] and your wilfulness [irada], in spite of your claim to be numbered among the loved ones [mahbubun] and those who have been drawn near [muqarrabun], this is a regrettable delusion that will hold you back and an unfortunate error that will lead you astray. If you realized that this world was sure to leave you in the lurch, you would not ask so much of it. When your inner [batin] becomes worthy to serve Allah, only then will this world become fit to serve you. Its wine is poison; it may taste sweet at first, but it soon turns bitter. Once it has filtered through into your heart and you have come under its control, it converts into a poison and kills you.

Our predecessors would learn to distinguish between different kinds of notions [khawatir], before withdrawing into secluded retreats [zawaya]. O you who cannot tell the difference between the notion [khatir] of the lower self [nafs], that of the devil [shaitan] and that of the heart [qalb], how can you withdraw into seclusion? The satanic notion prompts one to commit sins of disobedience and to make mistakes; it implants the root of unbelief [kufr], then encourages the sins of disobedience that branch out from it. As for the angelic notion [khatir al-malak], it prompts one to practice worshipful obedience and to perform righteous deeds.

Somebody said to him who was crucified (meaning al-Hallaj): "Give me a piece of good advice!" He replied: "It concerns your lower self [nafs]; if you can control it, [well and good], otherwise it will control you."

If you wish to drink in the company of kings, you had better take to the empty ruins, the wastelands and the deserts, until you sober up from your intoxication, so that you do not divulge their secrets and have them put you to death for it. This is why it is better for them [the people of the Lord] to go wandering about, rather than settle down. This world has been put here as a means of transport, if you wish to meet your Lord.

Seclusion [is appropriate only] after [observance of] all the rules of the sacred law [ahkam ash-shar']. The door of Allah (Almighty and Glorious is He) cannot be reached without seeking help, and a firm determination to achieve something will make the means available. The door of knowledge ['ilm] is arrived at by the path of the law [hukm]. The law means the [divine] commandments and prohibitions. We therefore accept what the law requires of us; we hear and we obey. At this stage we are exposed to adversities, so this is where the servant needs to be knowledgeable ['alim]. One of us may say: "Why should I have to suffer misfortune, despite my dedication to worshipful obedience?" Our response to him must be: "You need a little knowledge!"

The specialist in the law [sahib al-hukm] is concerned with storing the goods, while the specialist in knowledge [sahib al-'ilm] is concerned with their distribution. The law is associated with the pious abstainers [zuhhad], while knowledge is associated with the champions of truth [siddiqun], the loved ones, the intimate companions. Abstinence [zuhd] is associated with the law, while love is associated with knowledge. The one serves as a business partner [sharik], the other as a minister [wazir].

The ascetic [mutazahhid] is feverish [mahmum], the pious abstainer [zahid] is consumptive [maslul] and he who has real knowledge ['arif] is alive after death. This ascetic has renounced the desires of the flesh and has been fasting, so his lower self [nafs] has caught a fever. The pious abstainer has experienced prolonged renunciation, so his sickness has been prolonged and has caused him to contract tuberculosis. This world has died as far as he is concerned. While he is lying in this condition on the bed of the gracious kindness of Allah (Almighty and Glorious is He), what should appear at the door of his abstinence but food prepared in many different ways, as well as various styles of clothing hung on pegs! He cannot leave this world until he has received his allotted share in full. The unbelievers [kuffar] and disobedient sinners have not had the decency to seek [their proper due]; they have just helped themselves to things that are unlawful [haram].

Allah (Exalted is He) gave that servant life, then He resurrected him as a different creature. Flesh had withered away, bone had weakened, skin had grown thin. The lower self [nafs] had lost its sweet taste, passion [hawa] had departed and natural inclination [tab'] had been overcome, while the heart contained the spirit [ruh], the inner meaning [ma'na], the direct experience [ma'rifa] and the realization of Divine Unity [tawhid].

Complete dominion belongs to the heart alone, and the Lord of Truth takes care of it. He brings His servant back to life after his death, his carnal desires and appetites having died a spiritual [ma'nawi] death. A symbolic death along with an actual death. Allah brings him back to life after He has shown him what is over there. To the servant He has left dead at His door, He shows the vast scope of His wisdom and His mysteries, the multitude of His soldiers and His subjects. Then, when He has shown him His kingdom and informed him of His secret [sirr], He joins his spirit [ruh] to his body and his outer [zahir] to his inner [batin], so that he may receive his allotted shares [aqsam] in full. Prior to this, even if all the portions of the East and the West had been spread out before him, he could not have taken one single atom from them.

Through a mysterious power [qudra khafiya], an inner will [irada batina] exerted by Allah (Almighty and Glorious is He), His Prophets [anbiya'], His saints [awliya'] and the special few [khawass] among His creatures are detached from their worldly desires. Not the slightest trace of carnal desire and wilfulness remains within them, so that their inner beings [bawatin] are purely devoted to Him. Then, when He wishes to grant them their allotted shares in full, He creates the life of worldly existence [wujud] within them, so that all the allotted shares may be received.

Jesus (peace be upon him) did not marry; he never took a wife. At the end of time, Allah (Exalted is He) will send him back down to the earth, and He will then marry him to a young woman of Quraish, who will bear him a son.

As for the person with real experience ['arif], he does not receive his portion until after achieving proficiency in both knowledge ['ilm] and abstinence [zuhd], then he collects his allotted shares along with all the rest of you. He regains his worldly appetites after having abstained from them [to be on the safe side] whenever there was any doubt. Once he has acquired knowledge, cold water tastes good to him, while in the eyes of pious abstainers the finest meal seems like drinking wine and eating the flesh of the pig. Many a pious abstainer is shut off by his abstinence from the Lord of Truth, and many a person with real experience is shut off through dwelling too much on his experience [ma'rifa], although this is actually rather unusual and in most cases he is likely to be safe and sound.

As a general rule, your closeness to the sons of this world keeps you far away from Allah (Almighty and Glorious is He). The right course for you is to concentrate your attention on the hereafter and on worshipful obedience, then you may be saved, while your allotted shares will come to you even if they are unwelcome.

What He requires of you [first of all] is that you stop following your natural tendency [tab'] and put in its place the special concessions [rukhas] allowed by the sacred law [shar']. Then He will instruct you to give up these special concessions bit by bit, until all your actions are in accordance with the strict interpretation ['azima]. Then, if you patiently observe the strict version of the law, love for Allah (Almighty and Glorious is He) will arise within your heart. Once love is firmly established there, saint-ship [wilaya] will come to you from Allah (Almighty and Glorious is He).

If you are sensible, count yourself among the people of the Fire [of Hell], because this will encourage you to improve your conduct. If you are in fact one of the people of the Garden [of Paradise], you will have demonstrated your gratitude to Him. When you go out of your house, you should feel as if you were going forth to war, as if you might never come back home again. You should also be aware that you are made to suffer because of your acquisitiveness, and be convinced that Allah (Exalted is He) is capable of sustaining you without effort or strain.

The believer [mu'min] is sometimes like a mountain and at other times like a feather, blown about by the winds of His destiny [qadar]; in the face of misfortunes like a mountain, but in the company of the Lord of Truth (Almighty and Glorious is He) like a feather wafted by the winds of His decrees [aqdar].

O people of ours, it is too late for you to fill the role of Messenger [risala] or the role of Prophet [nubuwwa], but there is still time for you to experience saint-ship [wilaya]!

There can be no access to the King's company as long as one is still attached to worldly existence [wujud]. It seems you must be blind, since you do not see. It seems you must have quenched your thirst, since you do not drink. It seems you must be dead, since there is no movement in you. Woe unto the outcasts who are unaware of being outcasts! You do no good, nor do you help the good people to do good. You are bad; you love a worldly life with no hereafter, an outer [zahir] with no inner [batin]. You will gain no benefit from your important connections, your wealth and your patron. You will soon be dead, and after death you will suffer humiliation.

Should anyone desire glory, the glory belongs to Allah. (35:10)

And [thus it also belongs] to His Messenger [rasul] and to the saints [awliya'] and the champions of truth [siddiqun].

The ocean is this world, the ship is the sacred law [shar'] and the sailor is the grace [lutf] of Allah (Almighty and Glorious is

He). Anyone who deviates from following the sacred law will therefore drown in this world, but if someone seeks refuge aboard the ship of the sacred law and makes himself at home there, the sailor will appoint him to be his lieutenant [istanabahu]. He will put him in charge of the ship and everything aboard it, and will make him a relative by finding him a bride from his own family [saharahu]. This is how it will be for someone who forsakes this world, devotes himself to the acquisition of knowledge ['ilm], bears suffering with patience and comes to be the beloved [mahbub] of the sacred law. While he is in this condition, lo and behold, Allah (Almighty and Glorious is He) will come and bestow His grace upon him. He will grant him His intimate knowledge [ma'rifa] and invest him with robes of honour specially designed for him. One mark of divine friendship on top of another [wilaya fawqa wilaya]!

In Allah you have ample compensation for the loss of anything other than Him. If something happens to pass you by, do not feel sad about it, for the King disposes of His property as He sees fit. The slave ['abd] belongs to his Master [Mawla], along with everything he owns. Whatever He may take away from you, you will find it again tomorrow [at the Resurrection]. The Fire [of Hell] will say: "Pass through, O believer [mu'min], for your light has extinguished my flames!" Likewise in this world, when faith [iman] has grown strong and one's inner being [batin] has made contact with the nearness of the Lord of Truth (Almighty and Glorious is He), along comes the fire of disasters to cause an obstruction on the path of hearts. The fire of conflicts takes its stand on the path of aspirants, then it catches the aspirant [murid] because of the remnants he still carries, traces of worldly attachment and attention to creatures. To those of perfect faith [kamil al-iman] it says: "Pass through, O believer, for your light has extinguished my flames!" They are not injured in this world by arrows that fall from the castle walls. You must conduct yourselves in such a way that neither the fire of this world nor that of the hereafter will be able to harm you.

Allah (Almighty and Glorious is He) has certain servants whom He calls physicians [atibba']. He lets them live in good health ['afiya], causes them to die in good health and admits them to the Garden [of Paradise] in good health.

When someone really knows ['arafa] Allah (Almighty and Glorious is He), he becomes detached from carnal appetites and pleasures. It is only because he is compelled to do so that he accepts all his allotted shares [of worldly goods]. "The neighbour before the house [al-jar qabla'd-dar]." Having won the neighbour, this fortunate person [mubarak] now gains the house, established in possession by the King. The King has said:

You are today in our presence established and worthy of trust. (12:54)

When someone has really come to know Allah, and has been admitted to His presence, he will not reach out with his eyes or his hands toward anything in His kingdom. He is just like a bride ['arus] who has been solemnly escorted to the King. Her food and drink are the nearness of the King. In His nearness she finds the fulfilment of all her desires. When the lower self [nafs] has become obedient, it melts together with the heart, which becomes its jailer. Then the King releases the heart from the prison.

And the king said: "Bring him to me." (12:50)

After his nobility and his good character and good conduct have become apparent, he will be escorted into His presence. He will greet him with noble generosity, draw him near and bring him close, treat him kindly, invest him with robes of honour and address him without an intermediary, saying:

You are today in our presence established and worthy of trust.

He will keep all his attention focused on Himself.

MALFUZAT-3

IN EXPANSION [BAST] AND CONSTRICTION [QABD]

Question: When does expansion [bast] give way to constriction [qabd], and having fun to being serious?

As long as He is going easy on you [basataka], you can take it easy [inbasatta]. Then your license to enjoy concessions [rukhsa] will be converted into strict attention to duty ['azima], and then your strict performance will become a pleasure, until eventually, when the whole of you has become strictly devoted to duty, He will cause you to enter the abode of gracious favour [fadl] and intimate friendship [uns]. All that is left for you then will be action pure and simple [fi'l mujarrad], with no question of either concession or strictness. Your situation will be comparable to that of a person who has in front of him a dish containing a bit of food, and who is then told: "Go into a different house. Everything over there is for you." Concessions are for those who have made little progress, while strict requirements are for those who are fully developed [kamil], and the Kingdom is for those who have transcended this worldly existence [fanun].

Previously, I always dwelt here on earth in private seclusion, but now the situation is the very opposite of that. In general, I am a person who is not embarrassed by being talked about, because I take no notice of anyone's opinion.

Proper behaviour [husn al-adab] is called for in two instances: in the renunciation of this world and in the acceptance of it. You must not go into seclusion with ignorance for company. Do not make a practice of it before you are adequately prepared. "Complete your studies, then retire [tafaqqah thumma' 'tazil]." How often do you attend these sessions [majalis] without putting one word you hear into practice? How many of you have seen a single saint [wali], asked him for a piece of good advice, received such advice from him and then put it into practice, taking it as provision for your journey?

As for you there, you pore over the annals [akhbar], you peer into the traditions [athar], you attend the sessions of divine remembrance [majalis al-adhkar], yet you make no progress at all. If only you could hold your footing at the point you have already reached, but no, whenever you come forward you go into reverse.

If there is no difference for a person between one day and the next, he must be a dim wit. Come to your senses! May Allah have mercy upon you! This world can offer only momentary satisfaction, so do not rely on it.

There are some people who have been rendered weak by awe and dread, whose limbs have been rendered immobile and whose hearts have been overwhelmed by bewilderment at the creation, so that they have come to be a state of paralysis and inactivity. When the time comes for them to receive their full quota of allotted shares, Allah sends someone to feed them bit by bit.

No one past or present has anything to hold against this servant (meaning himself). Preserve the most important part of your religion [din], or else you must sever your connection with me and my path. Do not be an ignorant fool, sitting at home and indulging in your fantasies. Here we have medicines that we have drunk and found beneficial. Here we have something tried and tested, to which we can show you the way.

Beware of a day when neither wealth nor sons will be of any avail! What is wealth? Wealth is something you have accumulated from what has fallen due to you and what you have managed to acquire, and you have acquired it by any means. You claim that tomorrow [at the Resurrection] it will stand you in good stead, along with all the sons you have, just as the Arabs in the old days used to claim.

But Allah (Almighty and Glorious is He) has said:

The day when neither wealth nor sons will avail [any man], except one who comes to Allah with a whole heart. (26:88, 89)

Such a person will not have paid too much attention with his heart to his worldly goods and his sons. Rather than letting his heart rely on them, he will have recognized that he was entrusted with their care. He will have looked after them in order to comply with the wishes of his Lord. Thus his heart would be safe from the perils that come with having wealth and children.

Consider the case of a man who is informed that the king wishes to marry him to a slave girl, and that he intends to have him killed by her hand. The man says to himself: "If I try to run away, the king will catch me with his soldiers. If I refuse to obey him, he has the power to destroy me, but if I comply with his wishes, he will destroy me anyway, by means of his slave girl." The king does in fact command him to marry one of his slave girls, and he orders her to poison him or to slit his throat when he has fallen asleep. --Oh, how much is being missed by those who have stayed away from me today! Oh, how much they are missing! --But the best thing he can do is to behave politely and show himself ready to comply with the royal command, while keeping his heart on the alert. "To hear is to obey," says he, and in he goes to accept the marriage and the gift [hadiyya]. The wedding night [zifaf] has arrived. He dons the armour of caution. He anoints the eyes of his heart with the ointment of wakefulness, to make sure that he will notice her every movement, pause and action. She turns out to be his joy and delight, and the attendants and servants all think he must have found himself in an enviable situation. When the new day dawns, she has not murdered him with her poison!

...except one who comes to Allah with a whole heart [bi-qalbin salim]. (26:89)

This world is the wife in whose company he has not fallen asleep, and with whom he has never in his life been alone in private. He has reached the hereafter, and she has neither robbed him of his dutiful devotion [taqwa] nor altered his religion. That is keeping safe and whole [salama]! It is like this for one who really knows ['arif] Allah, who abstains from this world and yearns for the hereafter. The messenger of knowledge [rasul al-'ilm] comes into the pure serenity of his innermost being [sirr] with this information: "Allah wishes to assign to you a group of people from this world, so that there may be life for the hearts of the champions of truth [siddiqun]. This is a kind of task, one that requires labour and trouble and attention. Be careful how you perform it. Your heart and your innermost being [sirr] must be sound and whole, so the innermost being must be fully conscious of this." The innermost being and the heart are escorted together to the King's door. They ask: "What do You propose to do with us? Do You intend to exclude us from Your presence, to banish us from your door, to make life painful for us? We shall not leave without the proper assurances [mawathiq] and covenants ['uhud]." They will not leave until He says to them:

Fear not, for I am with you both. I hear and I see. (20:46)

Then they will return together to this world, accompanied by escorts and guards.

...except one who comes to Allah with a whole heart. (26:89)

[Such a heart is sound and free] from harmful influences, from pretence and hypocrisy and the desire to impress mere creatures.

O seeker far from home, O wanderer lost in the trackless wilderness of destiny [qadar]! You need to tidy up your private room. Leave in it neither dirham [silver coin] nor dinar [gold coin], and as for jewellery you have enough with the key in your pocket. You need to empty your heart of this world, of carnal appetites and pleasures and trivial concerns of every kind. You must let it contain only remembrance [dhikr] and contemplation [fikr], the remembrance of death and the remembrance of what lies beyond death. In it you must practice the alchemy [kimiya'] of curtailing expectation. You must say: "I am already dead," because actions become pure through the curtailment of expectation [qasr al-amal].

If you exaggerate your expectation, on the other hand, you will be seeking to make an impression on this person here, and behaving hypocritically toward that person there. Someone who has mastered the curtailment of expectation is separated from everything, disconnected from everything. He wears the garb of abstinence [zuhd], then the garb of annihilation [fana'], then the garb of real experience [ma'rifa].

Allah's Messenger (Allah bless him and give him peace) has said:

Guarantee me six things and I will guarantee you the Garden [of Paradise]: When one of you talks, he must not tell lies; when he is trusted, he must not cheat; when he makes a promise, he must not break it; you must restrain your hands [from evil deeds]; you must not look for trouble; and you must keep your genitals safe.

When your innermost being [sirr] has become pure and unified, you will hear the call of your Lord directly, without any intermediary. When your fear and your hope have been united, the speech of your Lord [Rabb] and Master [Mawla] will address you.

O my dear son, cast yourself down in front of the hoofs of the horse of His destiny [qadar]; it will either trample you or leap over you. "If someone suffers destruction [talaf] because of

Allah, his compensation [khalaf] is Allah's responsibility." If it does leap over you, catch hold of it and cling on, exposing yourself to the arrows of His destiny. When you become a target for the arrows of His destiny, their impact will only cause a scratch, not a fatal wound.

O you who are destitute of all this, you must improve, make progress and set to work. Get to grips with it all. Give up your bad habit of sitting at home while I am sitting down to give a talk. Here are the qualities of saint-ship [wilayat]. Here are the degrees [darajat].

O you who are afflicted with the burden of having dependants to provide for, let your earning be devoted to your dependants and your heart to the gracious favour of your Lord. For one group of people, their lawful goods [halal] are acquired though what they earn. There are people whose lawful goods are what they obtain in answer to their supplication [du'a']. There are people whose lawful goods are what they receive from others without having to ask, and then there are people whose lawful goods are what they get by begging. This is the state of affairs during training [riyada], which cannot go on indefinitely.

The first case, namely earning, is in accordance with the Sunna. The second, namely asking [in prayers of supplication], is of weak validity. The third, [accepting what comes without asking], is the approach that is strictly correct ['azima].

As for begging, this is allowed as a special concession [rukhsa]. It may happen that someone goes begging when he is not in need, in which case he represents a trial and a tribulation for the person asked to give. The request made by this servant [of the Lord] is like the request that comes in the night.

The Prophet (Allah bless him and give him peace) has said:

Do not reject the request that comes in the night, for someone who is neither a jinni nor a human being may come to you, in order to see how you are handling the blessings that Allah (Almighty and Glorious is He) has bestowed upon you.

In just the same way, this servant is commanded to ask, so that the Lord of Truth may see how you are handling the blessings that He has bestowed upon you.

Make a frequent practice of attending the sessions [majalis] of the scholars and of visiting the tombs and the righteous [salihun], then perhaps your heart will be brought to life.

Once they [the people of the Lord] have become thoroughly proficient in carrying out the commandments and observing the prohibitions [of the sacred law], the decrees of destiny [aqdar] come to their aid. 'Abdullah ibn az-Zubair used to eat one meal a week. Your spiritual state [hal] will not be correct until you are like a cracked pot in which no liquid can remain. Consider the example of the ship belonging to some poor folk, which was boarded by al-Khidr, who damaged it and then passed on to another situation. There is one state of being that features integration [jam'] and there is another that features differentiation [tafriqa], as there is one state that features paucity [qilla] and another that features multiplicity [kathra].

If someone goes out of my presence in the direction of the Fire [of Hell], may Allah have no mercy on him!

O Allah, pardon! O Allah, protection! O Allah, steadfastness! O Allah, contentment!

When you attain to the Lord of Truth (Almighty and Glorious is He), He will be satisfied with you as long as you perform the fara'id [obligatory religious duties, as distinguished from those that are merely commendable or supererogatory].

The King's cook is now an old man. No longer can he think, see, hear and give instructions [as he did in his prime]. He must now have done for him what he could do himself in his active condition.

Let Allah be your witness, O seeker, if you are speaking the truth about the claims you make. When have you ever used your strength for your neighbour's benefit rather than your own? When have you offered him your shirt, your turban and your prayer-mat [musalla] before using them yourself? When have you put your wealth at his disposal first of all?

These people [of the Lord] have dissolved their lower selves [nufus], their natural impulses [tiba'], their passions [ahwiya] and their tastes [sharab], to the point where they have died in the spiritual sense [ma'nan], where they have become extinct [fanu] in the spiritual sense. The hand of [divine] power [qudra] has taken control of them. The mortician [ghasil] of destiny [qadar] rolls them over to right and to left,

while their dog is stretching out its paws on the threshold. (18:18)

The remnants of the lower self are stretched out beneath the threshold of destiny.

The medication prescribed for the limbs and organs of the physical body is to refrain from sins [ma'athim]; that is to say, from perpetrating atrocious misdeeds and offences. Your hand must refrain from stealing and striking, while the foot must refrain from walking into sinful disobedience, and from walking toward the worldly ruler [sultan] or indeed any of the children of Adam. This eye of yours must be restrained from looking at pretty women.

The lower self [nafs] has become calm and quiet in the presence of the law [hukm]. The heart has flown off into the company of the Beloved [mahbub].

If the friend [wali] of Allah (Exalted is He) behaves correctly, he will acquire the attributes [sifat] of Prophethood [nubuwwa].

The law [hukm] fluctuates between nature [tab'] and knowledge ['ilm], sometimes rejecting nature and sometimes rejecting knowledge.

Whatever the Messenger gives you, take it. (59:7)

The law says to the heart: "What will supply your needs? I am standing at the ready, like a servant at your disposal, a guardian to look after you, while you are in the company of the King."

The night is their royal throne. The private retreat is their bridal chamber. The day excites their interest in certain material means [asbab].

Afflictions ought to be kept secret:

O my dear son, do not narrate your vision to your brothers. (12:5)

You must be strong in dealing with them. Protect one another and support one another until the book [of destiny] reaches its appointed conclusion.

Ask Munkar and Nakir about me when they come to visit you in your grave, for they will tell you all you need to know about me. Your present name is Mudhnib [sinner]. Tomorrow [at the Resurrection] your name will be Muhasab [called to account] and Munaqash [subject to interrogation]. In the grave you must suffer having all your faults exposed. You do not know whether you will be included among the people of the Fire [of Hell] or among the people of the Garden [of Paradise]. Your ultimate destination is uncertain, so do not overestimate the purity of your spiritual state [hal]. You do not know what your name is going to be tomorrow.

O my dear son, if you are still alive in the morning, do not take the evening for granted, and if you are here when evening comes, do not take the next morning for granted. Yesterday is past and gone with everything it contained, to be a witness for you and against you [when the Resurrection comes]. As for tomorrow, you do not know whether you will survive till then or not. You are simply the son of your today. How stupidly careless you are! The symptom of your heedlessness is your addiction to foolish company.

O stupid fool, why do you associate with those on whom the mark of the Truth [Haqq] is not apparent? Why do you seek the company of someone whose foundation is unstable, whose outer [zahir] is all lower self [nafs], and whose inner [batin] is all stubbornness and insolence toward the Lord of Truth (Almighty and Glorious is He)? This [business of ours] is not something that comes about through rubbing shoulders, nor through anointing the eyes with cosmetics [kuhl] but not with sleepless vigil.

The entire creation is of no consequence. All nonessential effort [takalluf] is of no consequence. O stupid fool, you go around begging from door to door, in order to accumulate a mass of worldly stuff. How can you have any hope of real success [falah]? Why not stand at the King's door like the chamberlain [hajib], informing the King of new arrivals, listening to their stories and making them feel less lonely? Why not treat your fellow creatures as your dependants, instead of depending on them? Why not work at your craft or profession in your own home, so that when they come to your door they will discover that you have something useful to offer them? Your home is your private retreat, your home is your heart, your home is your secret soul [sirr], your home is your inner being [batin].

To deserve the company of your Lord, you must carry out His commandments, observe His prohibitions and comply with His wishes by accepting whatever has been decreed [maqdur] by Him.

The blessings bestowed on your fellow creatures are in proportion to your prayer of supplication [du'a'] and your spiritual aspiration [himma], in the ratio of a thousand to one. When you honour the virtuous noble ones in your private retreat, you are obeying your Master [Mawla] and not offending against Him. If you honour the people [of the Lord] and do not disgrace yourself in their sight, you deserve to be called noble [karim]. Then, once you have come to be noble, a thousand individuals will be honoured for your sake. Misfortune will be averted from your family, your neighbour and the people of your town.

You are always begging. You are always going to people's doors. How long will it be before others can beg from you? How long before others can expect a meal from you? How long before they can come to your door? When will you be finished with your business? When will a tent be pitched around you? When will you celebrate your wedding in the close presence of the King? When will you demonstrate your excellence, your worthiness and your fitness for the proximity of the King? When will your titles [alqab] be made known and your magnificence be revealed? When will you be the noblest of the noblest of the descendants of Muhammad (Allah bless him and give him peace), so that his blessed grace [baraka] may be conferred upon you?

As the Prophet (Allah bless him and give him peace) has said:

The learned scholars ['ulama'] are the heirs of the Prophets [anbiya'].

[They are their heirs] in speech and in action, in spiritual state [hal] and in teaching [maqal], not in name and title. Prophethood [nubuwwa] is a name [ism], while Messenger-ship [risala] is a title [laqab]. O ignorant one, although Prophethood and Messenger-ship have passed you by, it is not yet too late for you to experience Saint-ship [wilaya] and attain to the stations of Ghawth [ghawthiyya] and Badal [badaliyya].

In the words of Allah (Almighty and Glorious is He):

Are you content with the life of this world, rather than the hereafter? (9:38)

The life of this world [hayat ad-dunya] is your lower self [nafs], your passions [hawa] and your natural inclinations [tab']. This is what is meant by this world-not carnal appetites [shahawat] of brief duration, for they are portions allotted to you by destiny [aqsam]. This world is what you take hold of with your own mental and physical powers [bi-himmatika wa-jawarihika]. What the King imposes upon you does not count as belonging to this world. Vital necessities do not count as belonging to this world, for you cannot do without a house to provide you with shelter, clothes to cover and protect you, bread to satisfy your hunger and a wife to make you feel at home. Living the life of this world means devoting one's attention to creatures and turning one's back on the Lord of Truth.

Passion [hawa] is at odds with rational contemplation [fikr]. Passion is at odds with worshipful service ['ibada]. The material means [sabab] is at odds with the Originator [Musabbib]. The outer [zahir] is at odds with the inner [batin]. Once you have mastered the outer, you will be commanded to master the inner. Once you have mastered the law [hukm] by putting it into practice, you will be His servant, you will be His follower, you will be His companion [sahib]. You will be constitutionally extinct to your natural inclinations. Knowledge ['ilm] will hold your reins, to keep you tightly in control. You will be like a husband between two spouses. You will be like the chamberlain [hajib] between the king and his chief minister [wazir]. You will be the beloved of this world and of the hereafter, of creatures and of the Lord of Truth (Almighty and Glorious is He) and the angels [mala'ika], a joy to all hearts.

We experience a state of being that is beyond your present awareness.

David said to his son Solomon (peace be upon them both, and upon all the Prophets [anbiya'], the Messengers [mursalun], the angels drawn near [to the Lord], the saints [awliya'] and the righteous [salihun]): "O my dear son, how vile is sinful error after humble submission [maskana], and how much worse than that is a man who used to be a worshipper ['abid], but who then abandoned the worshipful service ['ibada] of his Lord."

Are you content with the life of this world, rather than the hereafter? (9:38)

The life of this world is your personal existence [wujud], while the hereafter is your non-existence [fana'].

Our aspirations [himam] have a way of undergoing change, and our innermost beings [asrar] also have their way of experiencing transformation. The common people ['awamm] have a way of going through changes, and the special few [khawass] also have their way of experiencing transformation.

This world is what you can see, while the hereafter is that which is revealed [yuftahu] to you. You are presented with something you cannot comprehend, so you feel bewildered, but then all is made clear to you. When something presents itself to you as a matter of common sense ['aql mushtarak], it is of this world, but if something comes to you in terms peculiar to the intellect which is the intellect of intellects ['aql al-'uqul], then it is of the hereafter. Your innermost being [sirr] is otherworldly, while your outer [zahir] is this-worldly. The involvements of this world are with everything apart from the Lord of Truth (Almighty and Glorious is He), whereas, the hereafter is attachment to the Master [Mawla], and indifference to tittle-tattle [qil wa-qal], to praise and approval as well as to blame, and to the pursuit of self-interest. "Your interest is what is important to you [hammuka ma hammaka]."

If you are sincere about your purpose, the Lord of Truth (Almighty and Glorious is He) will take you by your hand. He will cause you to walk in the company of His destiny [qadar], and the strides you make will be longer than the strides of Adam (blessing and peace be upon him), because of the sincerity [sidq] of your purpose [irada], the excellence of your behaviour, and the way you turn a deaf ear to whatever your neighbours may have to say.

Let perdition befall you, O ignorant one, ignorant of the Lord of Truth, of the fact that His gracious favour is all around you, of the presence of His servants who have heard and obeyed!

The servant [of the Lord] sees his own allotted shares on the Preserved Tablet [al-lawh al-mahfuz], then he moves on to see the shares allotted to his wife and his children. Eventually, when he is lost in amazement, he hears a voice calling from his inner being [batin]:

He is only a servant on whom We bestowed favour. (43:59)

And surely in Our sight they are among the chosen, the excellent. (38:47)

This is something that comes about through preordainment [sabiqa]; it can then be purified by following in the footsteps of the Shaikhs.

MALFUZAT-4

ON WHETHER AND WHEN TO MARRY

The Shaikh (may Allah be well pleased with him) was deep in his state of rapture [sama'] and ecstasy [wajd], when he was handed a slip of paper with a question concerning a point of Islamic jurisprudence [mas' ala fiqhiyya] written on it. He said: "[I must ask you to wait] until I get permission to speak on the subject, and while I see what occurs to me." Then he said:

Is marriage a necessary duty [wajib], or not? On this question there is a lack of consensus [among the leading Islamic jurists]. There are those who maintain that dedication to worship is preferable, in the case of a person whose lower self [nafs] does not experience a strong desire [for sexual intercourse]. Such is the view held by ash-Shafi'i and Ahmad [ibn Hanbal], while according to Abu Hanifa there is greater merit in devoting oneself to marriage.

Where you are concerned, as long as you are a seeker [murid], it is more appropriate for you to concentrate on your worshipful service ['ibada]. If you are one who is sought [murad], on the other hand, it is not for you to manage your personal affairs; if He so wills, He will find you a wife, and if He so wills, He will keep you occupied in other directions.

If there is an allotment [in your destiny], you will obtain it in due course. The allotted portion [qism] will try to grab you by the tail, then it will say to the Lord of Truth: "Relieve me of my responsibility toward this fellow! He keeps running away from me, despite the fact that You have allotted me to him. What am I to do, since he will not pay any attention to me?" Then He will make you take notice of it.

As for the seeker [murid], marriage is unlawful [haram] for him from the point of view of the inner [batin]. Does he have a spare shirt to offer, or four inches of land? This is a traveller, whose only property is perseverance [thabat], not clothes [thiyab] and not furniture [athath]. He is actually stripped bare of all his own clothes. Once he has reached his destination, however, and his travelling days are over, if his King wishes him to take a wife, He will make him the owner of property; He can provide for him, as He can keep him deprived.

Anyone who makes friends with a fool must be a fool himself. The fool is someone who does not really know [lam ya'rif] Allah (Almighty and Glorious is He). He is content with the life of this world, rather than the hereafter.

O young man! Your allotted portion [qism] will not be used up by anyone else. Do not take your food from the hand of Satan and devour it to satisfy your natural urges [tab'] and your passions [hawa]. It is better for you to wait awhile, until you attain to your abode in the Garden [of Paradise], or to the nearness of your Lord.

MALFUZAT-5

ON CONNECTIONS [AWSIL]

Become connected [ittasil], then become disconnected [infasil], then make connections [awsil]. "Complete your studies, then retire [tafaqqah thumma' 'tazil]." If someone tries to worship Allah in a state of ignorance, he will do more harm than good. You must take along with you the lantern of your Lord's sacred law [shar']. By the light of the law [hukm], you will enter into the domain of knowledge ['ilm].

Stop depending on material means [asbab]. Part company with brethren and neighbours. As for the shares allotted by destiny [aqsam], it serves no purpose to abstain from them. Present your back to your wife. Present the allotted shares with your back. Act like an ascetic [tazahhad], then practice abstinence [zuhd] in earnest. Practice renunciation [i'rad] in earnest. Give up your greedy appetite. Refine your behaviour. You must be detached from everything apart from Him, dissociated from other creatures and from material means, always afraid that your lamp may go out and leave you permanently in the dark. While one is in this state, lo and behold, along comes the Lord of Truth with the oil of His providence to fuel your lamp. Your light is within your knowledge. To quote two sayings of the Prophet (Allah bless him and give him peace):

If someone puts into practice the knowledge he has already acquired, Allah will endow him with knowledge of what he does not know.

If someone devotes himself sincerely [akhlasa] to Allah for forty mornings, the fountains of wisdom [hikma] will gush forth from his heart onto his tongue.

While he is in this state, he will suddenly see the fire of the Lord of Truth (Almighty and Glorious is He). Just like Moses (peace be upon him) at the moment when he saw a fire, he will say to his household:

Stay here awhile. I notice a fire. (28:29)

The Lord of Truth will summon him by means of His fire. He will cause the fire to represent His nearness, and He will cause his vision of it to be his guide. When he sees a fire burning in the bush of his heart, he will say [to his household]: "Stay here awhile, right where you are now. I notice a fire." The innermost being [sirr] will call out to the heart:

I am indeed your Lord. (20:12)

I am Allah..., so worship Me. (20:14)

[In other words:] "Do not submit yourself to anyone but Me. Acknowledge Me and ignore all others. Become connected to Me and disconnected from everything apart from Me. Seek Me and turn away from all others, toward My knowledge ['ilm], toward My nearness, toward My kingdom, toward My dominion."

When you experience this completely, the meeting will finally take place. Whatever is meant to happen will happen.

And He revealed to His servant that which He revealed. (53:10)

The veils will be removed. Trouble and confusion will disappear. The lower self [nafs] will become calm. Peace [sukun] will arrive. The gifts of grace [altaf] will arrive.

Go to Pharaoh! (20:24)

"O heart, you must go back to the devil [shaitan], the lower self [nafs] and the passions [hawa]. Set them on the path to Me. Guide them to Me. Say to them:

O my people! Follow me. I will guide you to the way of right conduct. (40:38)

Become connected, then become disconnected, then become connected, then make connections [ittasil thumma'nqati' thumma'ttasil thumma awsil].

As for you, O miserable wretch, your strength and energy will soon run out and leave you in the lurch. Your bosom friends will have nothing more to do with you. You will experience the combination of poverty in this world and punishment in the hereafter. The grave will come and squeeze you so tight that one set of ribs is crushed against the other, rendering you incapable of responding to the questions posed by [the two interrogating angels] Munkar and Nakir. You will suffer agony in your grave, then a doorway to the Fire [of Hell] will be opened up for you, to let you be exposed to its torment and its toxic fumes.

O people of ours! Conduct yourselves properly in this abode [of the present life], so that your religion [din], your outer [zahir] and your inner [batin] may be kept safe and sound until you are made to stand before Him at the Resurrection. When that moment comes, the veil will be removed from your eyes, from your mouth and from your ears, and He will feed you and make you grow from strength to strength, from insight to insight, from life to life, from perpetuity to perpetuity, from blessing to blessing. He will commend your hard work and praise your good conduct. He will call you grateful [shakir] after He has called you patient [sabir], sensible ['aqil] and devout [dayyin]. He will cause you to experience further transformation.

Allah does not change what is in a people, until they change what is in themselves. (13:11)

Bad character is something they must change by following the sacred law [shar'], then knowledge ['ilm], then the decree of destiny [qadar].

It is as if they had been anesthetized [bunniju] in readiness for the amputation of their hands and feet, for the amputation of their rotten, gangrenous limbs. There is no movement, no asking about the whys and wherefores. All consciousness, all human consciousness is lost, until the days of anaesthesia [tabannuj] are over and consciousness returns to them. Then come the gracious favours of their Lord, to bring about transformation and further transformation. There is food to eat after hunger, something to drink after thirst, clothing to wear after nakedness.

As long as you are still following the path, He will command you to make do with very little, so that your carnal appetite [shahwa] may lose its intensity. You must give this ruling [hukm] its due, as you must be careful to observe all the commandments and prohibitions of the sacred law [shar'].

These days will come to an end, and your steps will draw near to the Lord of Truth (Almighty and Glorious is He) with the passing of the night and the coming of the day. They [meaning people who follow the spiritual path] are grouped in various categories: There are some for whom the entire journey takes only a day, while for others it may take a month or even several years. Instead of wasting your time on the whys and the wherefores and on speculating about the future, you should pull yourself together, get moving and get down to work.

If you labour in His palace, perhaps He will take you on as a permanent member of the staff. Maybe one of His slave girls will fall in love with you and you will marry her. Your outward appearance will be transformed. [Those labourer's tools of yours,] your basket made of palm leaves and your hoe can be sold off. You will be installed as a manager, a royal deputy and minister [wazir]. When someone really knows ['arafa] Allah, he does not regard such things as being too much to ask of Him. Once you have attained to Him, He will whet your appetite. Abstinence and renunciation are appropriate before direct experience [ma'rifa], before you attain to the King, before you know who you really are [qabla an ta'rifa man anta], what your title [laqab] is and what your name [ism] is.

The servant says goodbye to his worldly goods, to his clothes, his furniture, his home, his family, his children, his neighbours, his wife and his closest friends. He puts one foot forward and drags the other. With two steps, fear and hope, he moves away from the past. Nothing is familiar to him, for he is leaving everything behind, not knowing what he can expect or what may be expected of him. Then, once he has left everything behind, he arrives at the door of the King. There he stands in the company of His attendants, along with His riding animals, feeling both fear and hope, not knowing what may be in store for him. Meanwhile the King, who is watching him and has been informed about him, says to the attendants: "Give him special treatment, ahead of all the rest!" Then he gets to be employed in one post after another, until he is installed as a chamberlain [hajib] in His presence, as a special confidant who is privy to His secrets, invested with a robe of honour, with neckband, waistband and crown. Now he can write to tell his family:

Come to me with all your folk. (12:93)

After the King has called Himself as witness to His promise: "I shall not change toward you," he has a guarantee of constant companionship and friendship [wilaya], since abstinence [zuhd] cannot coexist with intimate knowledge [ma'rifa].

A case like this is one in a million. This is something that comes about as a result of divine destiny [qadar], preordainment [sabiqa] and foreknowledge ['ilm].

Do not be one of those concerning whom Allah has said:

No, I swear by the censorious self [bi'n-nafsi'l-lawwama]. (75:2)

The believer [mu'min] must ask, as a way of calling himself to account and improving his behaviour: "What did I intend by saying what I said? What did I intend by taking the step I took? What did I intend by eating what I ate? Why did I act as I did? Why did I do it? Is this in accordance with the Book and the Sunna?"

You must acquire certitude [yaqin] after self-examination [muhasaba], for it is the kernel [lubb] of faith [iman]. Only with certitude can the obligatory religious duties [fara'id] be properly discharged. Only with certitude can one put this world in its proper place.

When you receive a response to your supplication [du'a'], calm and composure, but if your prayer [da'wa] is not answered, you get upset! One of the distinguishing features of the champions of truth [siddiqun] is that they resort to Allah in every case. When they wish to conceal their spiritual states [ahwal], they may resort to the give and take of dealing with creatures, but their hearts remain with Him while their bodies are in the company of His creatures. The human being [ibn Adam] needs to work in this world, in order to transform his natural tendencies [tab']. He must struggle against his lower self [nafs], his devil [shaitan] and his passions [hawa], in order to move beyond the attributes of the animals [sifat al-baha'im] and acquire human characteristics [akhlaq insaniyya].

Do you disbelieve [kafarta] in this Lord,

Who created you from dust, then from a sperm, then shaped you as a man? (18:37)

Does He deserve as His recompense that you should deny Him and repudiate Him, that you should feel embarrassed to be seen by the eyes of other people, yet feel no sense of shame before Him, although He can always see you?

O you who make no secret of your claim to saint-ship [wilaya], while committing blatant sins of disobedience against the Lord of Truth! Do you feel no sense of shame before Him, when He is well aware of your innermost being [sirr] and your conscience [sarira]? And you there, you who make a display of poverty while concealing your wealth, are you not ashamed to be trading your religion [din] for your worldly interests?

Whatever blessing you enjoy, it is from Allah. (16:53)

Where is your gratitude?

O young man! Do not accuse anyone on behalf of your Creator. You are just as likely to be mistaken as you are to be correct [in what you suspect about another person]. Do not present other people in a bad light, in order to have Him approve of your own conduct. It is up to the sacred law [shar'], not our own minds, to determine whether a favourable or an unfavourable view should be taken. This is in relation to the outer [zahir]. You must also be careful to recognize cases where it is up to the inner [batin] to determine whether something merits disapproval or approval. The verdict [fatwa] of the heart can overrule the verdict of the jurist [faqih], because the jurist arrives at his verdict through some exercise of his ijtihad, whereas the heart always bases its judgment on what is strictly correct ['azima], on that which is pleasing to the Lord of Truth and in compliance with His wishes. This is the judgment [qada'] of knowledge ['ilm] over the legal ruling [hukm].

You must be servants of the law [hukm], then servants of knowledge ['ilm] while remaining in servitude to the law, in the sense that you must conform to it in humble compliance. You must enter along with knowledge into the company of the law. Any "matter of fact" [haqiqa] that is not acknowledged by the sacred law [shari'a] is an atheistic heresy [zandaqa].

When you enter into the company of the people of the Lord of Truth (Almighty and Glorious is He), you will experience what they experience and share the food they eat.

You must express your gratitude to Allah (Exalted is He) in secret and in private.

O people of this city, everything you are involved in is repugnant in my sight, just as everything I am involved in is repugnant in your eyes. We are opposites that cannot be reconciled. We manage to live amongst you thanks to the power of the Owner of the heavens, but there is no permanent residence here for the joy of our hearts.

Your youth has been spent in ways displeasing to the Creator (Almighty and Glorious is He). You are eager to please your wife, your children, your neighbour and your worldly ruler [sultan], yet you earn the displeasure of the angels [mala'ika] and the Lord of Truth (Almighty and Glorious is He), although:

...unto Him is the homeward journey [ilaihi'l-masir]. (5:18)

You are bound to answer the call of death. You will meet up with your fathers and mothers, brethren, friends and rulers. Let none of you ask: "When will the Resurrection take place?" For when you die you will experience your own Resurrection [qiyama].

The saints [awliya'] of Allah (Almighty and Glorious is He) are already there in the nearness of the Lord of Truth (Almighty and Glorious is He). They have lived their lives in a close relationship with the Lord of Truth. They have died many deaths: first of all to that which is unlawful [haram], secondly to that which is dubious [shubha], thirdly to that which is indifferently permissible [mubah], fourthly to that which is unambiguously lawful [halal tilq], and fifthly to everything apart from Allah (Almighty and Glorious is He). They are dead to all these things; they neither seek them nor come anywhere near them. They appear to have undergone a transmutation, turning them into inner contents [ma'ani] with no outer forms [suwar]. Then Allah (Exalted is He) revives them.

In the Name of Allah shall be its course and its mooring. (11:41)

When hearts are following a course that takes them across the oceans of destiny [qadar], their mooring is at the door of His knowledge ['ilm] and His nearness.

Wakefulness is a form of service, while sleep is a means of connection [wusla]. When the servant falls asleep during a ritual prayer [salat], Allah displays him proudly to His angels. The physical body is a cage and the spirit [ruh] is a bird.

In the eyes of the people of real experience [ma'rifa], creatures are like flies and hornets, or like silkworms. Their spiritual states [ahwal] have no relevance for you.

Be sensible! No one but a stupid fool would bring destruction upon himself to spite Allah; no one would do such a thing unless he was doomed to destruction anyway.

If someone tells you to be generous in spending and giving, that person is your friend. If someone gets rich on what belongs to the poor, he will be reduced to poverty because of it.

More is required of you than merely professing Islam. When will you put the truth into practice? When will you act on the truth?

When my limbs move, you should realize that my heart is aflame.

O world here below [ya dunya], taste bitter to My saints [awliya'] at the outset, so that they will not love you, but serve them later on, so that they will not be preoccupied with you.

When the Hour [of Resurrection] was mentioned in the hearing of Mary's son Jesus (peace be upon him), he would wail like a woman bereaved of her child, saying: "It is not fitting for the son of Adam to stay calm when the Hour [as-sa'a] is mentioned in his hearing." You are a nonentity. You have no feeling in you. You have never loved or been loved. He grieved over the length of his sojourn in this world, because it made him afraid of the fickleness of human beings, dependence on creatures, and separation from the All-Merciful [ar-Rahman] because of the dominating influence of the passions [hawa], the lower self [nafs], the natural impulses [tab'] and the devil [shaitan]. Anyone who feels secure in this world must be mightily ignorant indeed.

O young man! I am reassured, whatever may happen. I am made to feel afraid, whatever may happen. By my life, He draws you near and brings you close, He speaks to you, He feeds you and nourishes you, He watches over you, He opens doors for you, He seats you at the table of His gracious favour and His nearness, He puts you at your ease, but He still requires you to experience grief.